PA-LIWANAG

TO THE LIGHT

WRITINGS BY FILIPINAS
IN TRANSLATION

COMPILED BY

GANTALA PRESS

TILTED AXIS PRESS 2020
THANKS TO OUR KICKSTARTER BACKERS

INTRODUCTION

Gantala Press is an independent, volunteer-run, feminist small press/literary collective based in Metro Manila, the Philippines. We formed our group in 2015, initially as a response to the lack of women's voices in literary institutions such as workshops, seminars, and anthologies. As aspiring poets, we also wanted to have our works published. But even in this century there were no women's presses in the Philippines (although there still exist the NGOs and the university-based institutes or centers of women's studies that publish mostly academic journals). By the time mainstream publishers began publishing women's writings in the late 1990s to the early 2000s, the all-women literary collectives that flourished following the dark days of Martial Law (1972 to 1986) were already inactive.

We started the press about a year before Rodrigo Duterte came to power, but thriving in the time of Duterte could not have been more appropriate. Our first literary anthology came out in Women's Month,

2017. Later in May, the Marawi Siege against so-called ISIS-backed terrorists broke out. It so happened that one of the contributors to our first anthology was a Meranaw woman (who fled the burning city pregnant). So – as many women often are, to one another – we automatically had an involvement in, or a connection to, the issue.

We launched an information and fundraising drive for Meranaw women in July 2017 and held another session in August. Martial Law was declared in Mindanao. Another move to extend it to 2020 has been disapproved by the Senate. But in reality, as shown in the succeeding months and years, there is no reduction of militarization in the southern parts of the archipelago and the rest of the Philippines. Our engagement with the Marawi/Mindanao issue, and the realization that women are affected by social upheavals in different, specific ways, ushered our press to the political path.

When a government wages war against its people – surely a woman's press can and should do more than just publish books? When a president regularly cracks rape jokes, and the military intensifies its crackdown on activists, and the senate and congress enforce neoliberal policies that devastate the livelihood of farmers, the majority – surely a woman's press can and should call itself *feminist*?

We have since published the works of women farmers, plantation workers, nurses and migrant workers, and regularly contribute to fundraising efforts in support of factory workers on strike as well as urban poor communities. In this collection are writings by an arrested food factory worker; an urban poor community leader; a lesbian migrant worker; a former domestic helper; indigenous and peasant women; mothers, sisters, and daughters. We were able to source these works from the women themselves, after meeting them at people's fundraising events or writing workshops. The rest were responses to a call for submission to this project. Unlike most anthologies in the Philippines, many works come from writers outside of Manila, the capital. We made sure to include works from Visayas and Mindanao, the other major islands of the archipelago. Representative pieces from Gantala Press' publications from 2018-2019 were also included to clarify the social and political context of the collection, and the scope of the press itself.

We thank Tilted Axis Press for bringing these writings outside the Philippines, which has 170 or so languages. In this project, only four of those languages have been translated to English. Some pieces were even originally written in English, but are included here for carrying the spirit of the vernacular. Compared to other Asian or Southeast Asian countries, the Philippines does not really engage in translation – whether of foreign books to local languages, of local books to another local language, or local books to foreign languages. This book is our response to that gap.

As the reader journeys into this book, one may feel: darkness made conscious brings forth light. Works by women in this anthology still hold the pain and suffering passed on by those who came before them. We still speak about patriarchy and power, feudalism, capitalism, and imperialism. As we step into the second decade of the twenty-first century, we see a familiar mirroring of past events, all the way back to the eighteenth century Industrial Revolution and sixteenth century colonialisms. In this recurring loop, one may ask: What is true Liberation? The voices in this collection hint at simple yet profound answers, each writer humming a different note woven into one song. As words carry meaning on the spheres of the personal, social, and beyond, they offer beautiful renderings of the drama of life, as well as its transcendence. This is translation in its quintessential form. And this collection shows how women translate in translation.

The works here explain, illuminate – *paliwanag* – the darkness of the times. In Filipino, the prefix *pa* also means "to." And so, through translation – by themselves, or by other women – Filipinas bring these stories to light, *liwanag*, and emerge.

UNDIN

Nat Pardo-Labang

an undin lives in the girls' toilet
lurking at the back door of the last cubicle
feeling, waiting
everything that dangles
it devours

PUKI

Elizabeth Ruth Deyro

Why does a word feel dirty
no matter how hard I scour
it clean? I speak

in whispers, careful to pronounce
each syllable without making a sound,
afraid that someone will hear

and give my shame away. I look at myself
in the mirror as my mouth gives shape
to a word, bring the mirror lower and watch

the word become one with my body. I want to learn
a language where a word is not a word made
to sound violent, where a word is not a body

meant to be violated. I want to learn to speak
subtlety, the way I never learned
in any language that I know.

MEND

Roda Tajon
translated by Kristine Ong Muslim

When once my husband came home
with a rip in his pants
I shook my head in frustration, muttering:
this man is so sloppy!
I have learned to lament the loss
of things that have yet to outlive their
usefulness. Even when it is all right
to discard torn clothes, I will still look for
a matching piece of fabric to patch up
the tattered
pair of pants.

I welcome the eyestrain
from coaxing thread
into the needle's narrow eye.
Or, the pinpricked skin
of my finger. I don't mind
tear-shaped blood drops squirting
each time I prick my fingers when stitching—
I will wipe the blood away again on the shoelace, the waist
the pocket and back part of the garment as reminder
of my refusal to sew up
what continues to be
slashed open.

THREE POEMS

Christine Marie Lim Magpile

I. DON'T PAPA

(to the tune of "Bakit Papa?")

Uuuyy!
Papa is alcoholic, daring.
Papa is troublesome, broke some glass.

Papa, don't you love Mama?
Too bad, she is beautiful and kind.
Even if you are lazy and a wife beater,
Mama did not leave you for another man.

Papa, why do you hurt Mama?
But look at you, you are a slob sloth.
You spend more time with your drinking buddies.
Papa, please do not come back anymore.

Mama always has bruises.
You constantly swear.
Why do you still hope, Mama?
Please, Mama, fight back.

II. DESAPARECIDO

(to the tune of "Despacito")

Ah, police.
Oh no! Hurry.
Faster, run!

Desaparecido.
Where is Mama mia?
Arrested like a prisoner
Even if Mama's a kind person.

Desaparecido.
Mama is already desperate.
But the lawyer cannot take action.
When I grow up, I will be a rebel.

III. WHERE HAVE YOU BEEN?

(to the tune of "Saan Ka Man Naroroon")

Where have you been, Mother?
You've been in Arabia for so long.
I might not recognize your face.
My heart longs for your love.

When are you coming home, Mother?
My dream is to give you a kiss.
There was news this afternoon.
My memory of mother,
Here remains in a coffin.

FIVE-TO-TEN MINUTE OPERATION

Carissa Natalia Baconguis

Consider the mango tree,
bearing fruit in the summer, how the unripened
sells cheap in Philcoa; think of the sourness, not
the soreness of opening. Consider

last New Year's, we burned a tree
as an accident. Think instead of your job,
of translation, of the fruity smell of alcogel,
simply allow the stick

in your ass. Consider the movement of running,
the body revealed. Don't think of tiredness, because
you are tired. Trust the faithful bruise,
the proof that you didn't really want this. Think

of longing, of translation: that each day
is a translation of what you cannot say. And after
you translate, you begin to explain: yesterday
on the street I found a cat stiffening, laid down,

face smashed and being eaten by the flies, limbs
    stretching
as if reaching. Reaching or gripping a knife, the last
memory of body in desperation transcends death.
I wonder if I am crazy for connection,

like whenever I say I don't want children
in family reunions, or when I am the reason
they feel political and youthful. The untiring
let's forget it! Stretch or die, evolution or death! Tired

of my mother, of my father, of my sister, of my brother,
of my teachers and my old teachers, of my priests,
of my sacristan crush, of my babaylans, of my
neighbors, of my friends, of my old friends, enemies,
enemies of enemies, of Bathala, of celebrities, of
authors, of artworks, of self, of mangoes, of the two
mangoes born, or oranges, in the holy, in the dirty,
of Maria, of tiredness, tired

now of everything but don't
think of this too. Consider that you
don't believe you can be loved
so you settle instead in usefulness.

Yet you want to love, you try
to love, and something slips out,
as violent as it had entered, and
as lacking as the swelling of the inside.

If it is longing you are looking for,
it is not here in the hollowness of your being,
in the operation fucking your ass. Teach your body again
that you are able still to be generous.

And if my own existence
is action, if hollowness is paradox. If
I am full of shit, and when you pull
you get shit on you, if

my body realizes that it no longer wants
to be what I want it to be,
maybe I'm responsible for my own grief?
My own weakness

is a bridge. Woman is the definition
of paradox. I am a bridge
to womanhood, to manhood, to the revolution
of others, to fear. Don't take me away

from the holiness under the fruit. Because that's where
everything is, right? The two fruits are metaphors
of the privilege of choice. Everything I have
is here, in the ripening of existence. So, fuck—

it is painful to wait. So I lie down,
and open my legs. I remind myself to breathe
in the doctor's office. And while I wait for results,
I only stare at the bathroom mirror,

fixing my eyeliner. Everything,
even disgust, will come
but later. At least let it be
later.

ONCE I HAD ASKED HER

China De Vera
translated by Kaisa Aquino

Once I had asked her:
"Naa kay kalintura?"
Who else will not be mistaken
to be shivering
if she wrapped herself
with new old clothes,
all uncut ethics and parts
brushing her darkened nape
from long hours of grass cutting
in the banana plantation
as old as her grandfather.

It's not that
she fears not being
seen in the dark.
Neither is it
that her body had befallen
some sort of illness.
She is merely preparing herself
for when they flee.
Someone whispered to her last night:
"The helicopters will be back tomorrow,
and they will bring bombs."

MOTHER AND HER GHOSTS LEFT HANGING IN THE YARD

Kaisa Aquino

My mother, alone in her bed now, wakes in the middle
  of the night.
Outside, the wind howls and the moon is the shape of
  the bottom
of a candle that has spent the length of its wick trembling
  with light.
She sits up tentatively and looks out the window only
  to make out
a shape that appears to be waving to her, a body moving
  gently first,
then urgently.

"Lakay ko," my mother whispers, calling my father by
  the name she
had picked for him, which simply means, my man, my
  old man,
reaching out a hand to the window, to the shape outside
  looking at her.
It begins to rain, the wind howling louder and just then,
  the clothes
she had left forgotten on the laundry line went
flying down the yard.

THREE POEMS

Liberty A. Notarte-Balanquit

SWITCH

Darkness comes home
in a switch: a ritual

she garbs her firstborn in nightwear
and, until the second child yawns,
she battles with some naïve interrogation:
when will you die?

as she bargains
for a little patience

the night veils
the bedroom and
for a moment
the mother gathers
another piece
of herself.

A GIFT OF SUSPICION

The mother is always warned
by the perils of dusk

so she masters
her suspicions
by the thump
in her chest

she tugs the rosary
between her fingers
to drag the sacred
hour:

The First Joyful Mystery.

BIRTH

For Randy Felix Malayao

A fraction of a mother's soul

is set for the final
abdominal spasm
and force
to deliver
a world

and a portion of it
is in your blood
seeping into the ground
growing thousands
of mountainous wombs
to labor your birth.

Translations of poems in Pira-pirasong Pilas: Mga Tula *by Liberty A. Notarte-Balanquit, Sentro ng Wikang Filipino, 2019*

I WISH

Yolanda F. Catalla

We lacked stuff, my child—
plastic plates were scratched; forks, spoons if there were any, are twisted, bent.

We dreamed of simple relief: rice and viand
in the kitchenette, rent ready at month's end;
no bill collector at the door.

"You don't have a Mom!" your classmates said. You've asked,
"Where is Mom?" If we talked, I would've told you that I, too,
wanted to roam a mall, eat Chicken Joy at Jollibee;
that I got tired of cleaning other people's homes.
I wanted to see you in school, continue to high school, maybe college.

Lack—the excuse for leaving you caused a breach between us that can't be erased, repaired. Though we now have food in the new ref, a flat screen in the living room of our small home, I pursued my rainbow at a cost. I wish you could forgive me for my cowardice, for my neglect of you.

       I love you, my child.
I wish you knew.

PIA WURTZBACH AND I

Karla Quimsing

When Steve Harvey announced that Miss Colombia won the Miss Universe beauty pageant, we airline passengers were informed for the nth time that our flight had been delayed. I hadn't even finished cursing when he withdrew his statement and declared that the real winner was Miss Philippines. Unbelievable! And what timing, an announcement boomed again that we could now board the propeller plane and fly to our destination. So I slowly stood, wearing the baby bag like a sash. I lifted up my two-year-old with my left arm like a bouquet, and with my right hand held my five-year-old, who trailed behind me like a cape. Then the ground steward approached me, and ushered me and the children forward before everyone else in the long winding line. I looked back and saw on the TV monitor our Miss Philippines, Pia Wurtzbach, with her mouth open, aghast! I don't know if it's just coincidence, but when Miss Colombia wept, a heavy rain poured down on the runway of Mactan. I imagined the crowning of Pia when, this time, three airline crew assisted me, one holding an umbrella over my head. So, I go! I sashayed up the airplane in my imaginary high heels! Just like a beauty queen, I felt like crying too. What else can I do? But to fly a kiss, wave, and whisper, "Thank you! Thank you!"

RETURN

Karla Quimsing

Before leaving her exile in Honolulu, Mrs. Marcos, a prodigious collector of shoes, gave a demonstration of her style—taking off and brandishing a white, size eight Charles Jourdan shoe with a gold ornament and declaring that she was ready to resume her role as "a symbol, a standard for the Filipino people, something like a Miss Philippines." – The New York Times, Nov. 4, 1991

The wind blew a quiet storm
breaking off a ripening guava
from a branch of an aged tree
that can be seen from the window
of a lonely room.
Not a waft was felt
by the dictator's coiffed widow
inside an airplane from Honolulu.
She stares at her shoes, praying
as she descends to Manila.
Just as her sole hits the tarmac,
the guava explodes on the hardened soil.
Flesh and skin and seeds spilling.
The fresh scent of decay rises
blown into the window
of the lonely room
where a mother is dreaming

about her daughter
who disappeared during a protest rally.
She saw her little girl standing
under the guava tree
staring at the window.

SISTER AND BROTHER

Miriam Villanueva

translated by Faye Cura

It is four in the morning.
The rooster is crowing.
Big sister gets up from the bed,
Mother is nowhere to be found—
she has already gone out to sell.
Big sister's movements are quick.
The striking of the match,
the feeding of wood into the stove.
The washing of rice in the pot
before placing this on the stove.
The sweeping of the floor
while keeping an eye on the rice.
She goes out to harvest banana leaves.
The rice is now being kept warm on the coals.
Big sister skewers the dried fish and roasts these on the coals.
She draws rice from the pot. The dried fish is now cooked, too.
She feeds the fire once more
and lets it lick the leaves.

It is five in the morning. She calls to her brother,
"Get up!"

while she wraps the rice
in the leaf, along with the fish,
their packed lunch in school.
Sister and brother eat together.
Then, they bathe at the nearby water pump.

It is six in the morning. Their feet race
towards school,
sister and brother, children of farmers.

TIEMPO MUERTO

Rae Rival

Fifteen days of work for a thousand
during boom of harvest.
Fifteen days of work for a hundred
during tigkiriwi—crisis period.

Nanay Lani takes home two
twenty peso bills and a pocket-sized
paper bearing a list of borrowed rice,
noodles, soap, and canned food
from the landlord's sari-sari store.

During kabyaw—milling season,
Nanay Lani takes home a thousand
for selling sugarcanes in bulks.
Night watchers and grass cutters
are non-productive so they are paid
two hundred to five hundred every
fifteen days during tiempo muerto—
dead season.

PASIG JAIL

Melanie dela Cruz

translated by Faye Cura

How sorrowful our experience
Inside Pasig Jail
Surrounded by walls
Iron bars in front of us

The cause of our imprisonment,
We set up a strike at work
Two decades we were taken advantage of
That's why

At four in the morning, we're already up
So the mayora wouldn't yell at us
We endured a cold bed
Slept without a pillow or blanket

We suffered behind bars:
We were slaves, made to wash the piled-up dishes
We ate spoiled rice
Just so our stomachs wouldn't be empty

We are fighting for our wages and rights
But we were taken by bribed policemen
We workers were the ones imprisoned

While the real criminals run free

We workers were the ones imprisoned
While the real criminals run free

CHALLENGE

Estrelita "Ka Inday" Bagasbas
translated by Rae Rival

Though my eyes are failing
I still see the oppressive system
I do my share because I desire
That this rotten society be changed.

My hearing may be weakened
But I still hear
The call and the struggle,
I am for a free society
So I am at the forefront of the real struggle.

Though my feet ache with arthritis
I walk the streets as a promise
Aware that I must trudge on for freedom
With the ultimate aim to end imperialism

Weakness and limitation cannot be a hindrance
I carry freedom
Onward I go
I strengthen my stand for my country's liberation

So I challenge the youth,
To change the system
Of our decaying society,
Join Save San Roque Alliance!

WE, THE POOR

Organisasyon dagiti Nakurapay nga Umili ti Syudad (ORNUS)

We the poor
Toil daily
Doing the heaviest labor
But receiving the lowest wages

Pity us, the poor
Where can we find jobs?
We walk until evening
Seeking employment

There are contracts
Let's go do some shoveling
Even if we earn just a little
It's better than getting charged with estafa

Collect bottles
Plastic, paper and cans
To sell when their prices climb
We'll have something to survive on

Sell vegetables
Fruit, clothes and foodstuff
Just take caution
That they don't catch you

Sweep streets
Fill the water drums of the rich
Wash their clothes
Clean their houses

We people will take
Any kind of job
We will put up with, make do with
Small wages

Poor compatriots
Join and persist in
The movement for
National democracy

Dongdong-ay, sidong-ilay
Insinalidumma-ay
Dongdong-ay, sidong-ilay
Insinalidumma-ay

Reprinted from KALÍ: Voice of Cordillera Women, *Vol. XIII No. 1, Cordillera Women's Education Action Research Center, Inc., December 2018*

MY WORLD

Judy Cariño

My world – water, earth
Wind, gold, fire

They twist the truth, hide reality
They do not want their dirty secret to be revealed
Their great sin against all of Mankayan
And the village along the river

Poisonous chemicals dumped in the water
Mine waste dumped directly into the water
How many dams have collapsed during storms?
Nothing grows in silted rice fields

Heed the warning, this place is hazardous
Caused by underground excavations, the surface is sinking
The schoolhouse in Mankayan poblacion is in ruins
A big chunk of Colalo is gone, what sort of calamity will follow?

What's the smoke, it has a nasty stench?
Plants are wrinkled, fruit rots
What is this I feel? I have difficulty breathing
My neighbor has recurring bronchopneumonia

The company extracts profits in billions

But its miners receive wages hardly enough to live on
When the workers went on strike, this unyielding company
Had their march strafed with bullets

They will be faced with the fire of the mass movement
The anger of workers, peasants, minorities
Enough is enough, stop expanding
Stop Lepanto's destructive mining

Reprinted from KALÍ: Voice of Cordillera Women, *Vol. XIII No. 1, Cordillera Women's Education Action Research Center, Inc., December 2018*

LET'S GO

Judy Cariño

Let's go, compatriots
Let's go, comrades
Let's go, my friends
Let's go

Rise up early
Bring the children
Pack some food so that no one gets hungry
The trip to the village will be a long one
Be careful at AFP[1] checkpoints

Bathe in the river
Line up for food
Cook for thousands of people
Teach and learn, ask and speak
Sing wassani, salidummay, kulilipan

Embrace comrades
Exchange stories
Remember the heroes and martyrs of the struggle
Wave flags, long live the people of the Cordillera
Fight for life, honor and ancestral land

---

1   AFP – Armed Forces of the Philippines.

Reprinted from KALÍ: Voice of Cordillera Women, *Vol. XIII No. 1, Cordillera Women's Education Action Research Center, Inc., December 2018*

TWO POEMS

Eileen R. Tabios

SCUMBLE-D

—*after "The Bounty" by Derek Walcott*

I cannot remember the name of that mountain city
but it trembled

..............................it is near XYZ
a town with hyphens

Now, so many deaths

..............................the only art left—
the preparation of grace

THE FIRST FACE TRANSPLANT

After Imee Marcos

A dog mauled
                her

Surgeons repaired
her with someone else
                's face

The face donor is rumored
to have committed suicide

Successful surgery
But she can't purse lips

                into a kiss

                that kiss

LABYRINTH

Priscilla Supnet Macansantos

I am pure innocence
Swept by my seeking
Into the corral of this knowing
To take in
The metaphysics of desire
The politics of acquiescence
The aesthetics of color
The measure of the eye of the needle.
I am the incautious seeker
Drawn by the seemingly profound wisdom distilled
From uncountable pages
And I was enchanted by the magic of rhetoric
The fragrance of brittle paper
And I became intoxicated.

I am the seed nurtured
In the nest of metaphors,
Adventurer looking out to discover
That mud is darker than coffee
And extreme hunger finds its way
Through the eye of a needle
Because the gods are cold,
Cold marble statues
And my wine, my metaphysics
Politics

Aesthetics
Mathematics
Are mere shreds of sterile lifeless pages
Here in the labyrinth of meaninglessness
Home to worn-out spirits, slumbering,
Self-assured
In the hollow knowledge
Regarding man
And god
About transgressions
Of man against man
Of man against god
(Of god against man.)

TO E. S.

Priscilla Supnet Macansantos

No love is truly proper
Or wrong.

One who loves
Can be selfish
And meddlesome
Generous, yet oftentimes needy
Trusting, but given to doubt
And suspicion.

How does one prepare
Love's cup of coffee
If too potent, love is utterly bitter
Yet when lacking in strength
Love does not waken one from slumber.
When exceedingly sweet, love quickly
Loses its appeal.
And if terribly hot
It burns the mouth
And the belly,
But when not enough heat remains,
Oh love,
Is this coffee, truly?

But love is not just

A cup of coffee
That one pours down the drain
When lacking in heat. No.
One schools love
In just the right warmth,
Pacifies it when there is much heat,
Coaxes it back when warmth leaves.
And when it intrudes inordinately
One restrains love,
Holds it back at the doorway.

Love is a warrior
When faced with danger and hardship,
In times of drought and weakness
One fosters love, keeps it alive.

No love is truly right
Or wrong.
No.
One neither measures
Nor examines love.

The fitting question
Is, in times of storm
And difficulty
Is Love cowed? Does it flee
Or does it stay to fight the battle?

I KNEW THE WAY TO YOUR HEART

Dumay Solinggay

I knew the way to your heart
because your raspy voice spelled rugged roads,
of mothers protesting naked against colonizers,
of a calm lake,
and of the scent of cardamom in my chai.

In a different landscape, I have made this journey, too.
This led us to reach the airport
where our departure gates were separated
by eons of walking and surviving, struggling and dreaming
in the land and seas that Kings and administrators
bordered on the map with the name Southeast Asia.

When we punctuated the memory of soul-chilling separation
with a kiss, I knew I had reached home.
But I can only do so much.
The familiarity I learned in your presence
will fade away like time, like airplanes departing.

I knew the way to your heart,
but to stay there I can only do so much.
I can only improve my skills: reading maps, strengthening my voice,

sticking incense in the earth and praying for a better morrow,
re-learning the past,
disobeying Kings who decreed what is foreign and what is not.

SIKA

Ilay L. Quidangen

I loved you in my mother tongue
a language that does not drip or flow
with all its gnashing consonants: the *k*s and
the *t*s and the *n*s, and hard, stern vowel sounds
tripping the tongue like rocks and boulders
riddling the Karayan Buaya in the summertime,
daradar, kalgaw; see? But you already know that.
It was the language that welcomed you
into the world, the one that raised you.
I grew with it very differently.
I didn't know softness in it,
endeared only with borrowed phrases.
Thrilling to realize it now, you showed me
how the coiled sounds of *g* and *ng* are also
tender with unbridled warmth:
dungdungwen, isu nga kagasat, ingungoten
in the language I only knew how to
grieve, and mourn, and unravel—
leddaang, liday, panagladingit—
you introduced me again to familiar words,
reacquainted me with their affection
now they are so very familiarly felt—
dungngok, patpatgek, ingungotek.
Everything to do with you I now say in the past tense—
I loved you, you must know that,

and I have missed you
Mailiwak kenkan ken kailiwkan, ngem
To say "*agkitatanto*" is no longer true
To say "*agkitatanto pay*" will now always be untrue
in this lifetime, *napaay nga kari*
Iti iriringkuas ti dungdung-aw, ununnoy di latta
maibulosan; rakep-rakep, apungolko't
ladawan ti isem ken katawam
iti natalingenngen nga ayatmo, haan nga
kimmapuy uray kimmapuyen 'tay
pananggemgem mo ti imak.
Here I am, in the past tense, speaking in this
foreign tongue of foreign tongues
more fluent now in my first language not only with
its form and build but in all its spirits.
Everything to do with you I now say in the past tense
I still cannot write about you fully in Samtoy—the landscape
in which I truly saw you and you truly saw me
without a moment of flinching.
In this after your heart remains
with you I learned to feel, to become
in the language that raised me to be then unbecome.
I learned to love: *ayayaten ka*—no, that's not right.
Inayat ka.
Once again, after this loving, I grieved.
I have also mourned.
Here we are,

tungpal. Udi. Ungto. Kagibos.
Ipapas mo't aginanan, dungngo.

YOU

Ilay L. Quidangen

I loved you in my mother tongue
a language that does not drip or flow
with all its gnashing consonants: the *k*s and
the *t*s and the *n*s, and hard, stern vowel sounds
tripping the tongue over like rocks and boulders
riddling the Karayan Buaya in the summertime,
dry season, summer season, see? But you already know that.
It was the language that welcomed you
into the world, the one that raised you.
I grew with it very differently.
I didn't know softness in it,
endeared only with borrowed phrases.
Thrilling to realize it now, you showed me
how the coiled sounds of *g* and *ng* are also
tender with unbridled warmth:
dearest, my life partner, beloved
in the language I only knew how to
grieve, and mourn, and unravel—
sorrow, melancholy, to mourn—
you introduced me again to familiar words,
reacquainted me with their affection
now they are so very familiarly felt—
my dearest, my precious one, the one I love dearly.
Everything to do with you I now say in the past tense—

I loved you, you must know that,
and I have missed you
I miss you and I long for you, but
to say *"we'll see each other"* is no longer true
to say *"we'll see each other again"* will now always be untrue.
In this lifetime, *unfulfilled promise*
as the wailing bursts out of me, I still cannot let go of
my own cries; I clasp, enclose with me
the image of your smile and laughter
your earnest love, that did not
waver even when your grasp
of my hand had weakened.
Here I am, in the past tense, speaking in this
foreign tongue of foreign tongues
more fluent now in my first language not only with
its form and build but in all its spirits.
Everything to do with you I now say in the past tense.
I still cannot write about you fully in Samtoy—the landscape
in which I truly saw you and you truly saw me
without a moment of flinching.
In this after your heart remains
with you I learned to feel, to become
in the language that raised me to be then unbecome.
I learned to love: *I love you*—no, that's not right.
I loved you.
Once again, after this loving, I grieved.
I have also mourned.

Here we are
ended. In the last moments. The end. No more.
Rest fully now, my dearest.

HENS IN THE CULL: WOMEN IN THE TIME OF TOKHANG

Abbey Pangilinan, Mixkaela Villalon, Ica Fernandez

You see it in poultry farms. Brood hens whose eggs are allowed to hatch into chicks exhibit a maternal instinct so particular that the English language has an idiom for it. Mother hens raise their chicks protectively. They give up their own security to protect the survival of the brood. When strangers enter the coop, mother hens puff up in anger, completely covering their chicks from potential predators. This instinct is so powerful that a hen will unthinkingly protect chicks from another brood if its mother is not around.

The mothers of Sitio Pagkakaisa in Pateros, the place whose muddy riverbanks are renowned for their balut and itik, know all about the mother hen instinct. For the first six months of the Duterte Administration's so-called War on Drugs, 19 out of the 28 killings in

Pateros were in their neighborhood—an alarming jump from the previous one homicide per year.

Since then, the women of Pateros organized themselves to stop this threat to the lives of their husbands and sons. After cooking dinner and doing household chores, Merlia Balana and her neighbors would start their nightly ronda. Fueled by coffee, biscuits, and motherly rage, these women walk the streets with nothing but flashlights, telling off drunks, and making sure that no assassins riding motorcycles in tandem could kill members of their families while they slept. These women may be losing sleep but there have been no Tokhang-related deaths in Pateros since January 2018. This is just one picture of how women are responding to the various facets of the drug war.

It is difficult to tell just how many people have been killed as a result of the Duterte Administration's flagship program. Data collected from news reports in the past two years suggests approximately 28,000 extrajudicial killings. In official reports, among the "accomplishments" listed by the Philippine government are the 4,279 casualties killed in police operations. Some 22,983 cases are classified as deaths under investigation (DUI), or deaths in the war on drugs that were outside "legitimate police operations."

As of May 2018, official police reports state that 1.3 million drug suspects have surrendered, while 143,335 have been arrested. These are all conservative estimates. The actual death toll could be much, much higher.

EMPTY NESTS

The Philippine drug war, popularly known as Oplan Tokhang (derived from the words "knock" and "plead" in Cebuano), has established a pattern in which almost 95% of the victims are men. Whether middle-aged or in their teens, almost all have been from urban poor communities throughout the country. This, however, does not mean that women are safe from the violence. From the early days of Oplan Tokhang, the narratives of mothers, wives, and grandmothers revolved around their lost loved ones. Reports barely featured them as targets. It was not until recently that the death of Jennifer Taburada, whose husband was one of the thousands killed in the drug war, also raised the alarm of women becoming targets of state-sanctioned murder.

Mary was nursing her youngest child in her home when bonnet-wearing assailants barged in. Their real target was her husband. Known in the community as a drug addict, he was on the roof of the house when the attack took place. When the killers burst through the door, Mary flung her baby away before she was shot four times in the head—a clear case of palit-ulo, or substituting one target for another to reach a quota. The masked killers then ordered Mary's four older children to clean up the crime scene. Mary's eldest daughter recounts picking her mother's teeth up from the floor.

Mary's wake was held in a church-owned property not far from the family's residence. Her husband, who made a meager living selling binatog, surfaced briefly during the wake to leave flowers on the coffin. The barangay's anti-drug-abuse council still has an open case on him, alleging that he ran a drug den. Since their mother's death and their father's disappearance, Mary's five children have been separated to be cared for by distant relatives.

In another case, 17-year-old Angel, one of seven children, dropped out of school and ran away with her boyfriend Jerico. Angel and Jericho began living together despite her father's disapproval. Angel wanted to finish her schooling, and Jericho was supportive enough to split his earnings as a construction worker to buy her uniforms and school supplies. The couple were last seen together along Gumamela Street in Litex, where they were shot six times by unknown gunmen. Angel was found atop a pile of rubbish. She had a Barbie doll in her back pocket—a gift for a younger sibling. Jerico was not on the drug watchlist. His and Angel's deaths count as a "death under investigation." Their families had to raise 58,000 pesos to claim the couple's bodies from the morgue and give them a proper burial.

THE HENS AND THE FOXES

Most of the male victims of the drug war were breadwinners. They worked subsistence jobs but still managed to be providers. The deaths of these men have left behind not only grief, but also the grim responsibility of providing for their families. Given the poverty and relative lack of education of these wives, mothers, and grandmothers, being able to raise enough money to support these children, let alone navigate the male-dominated Philippine legal system, is unthinkable.

Lorna tells the story of her son, Romeo, who asked for her blessing to sell drugs. Romeo wanted to make money to build a house and to have Lorna's cataracts operated on. Romeo looked at the larger houses in the neighborhood, pointing out that there was only one lucrative source of income available in their urban poor community. "Hindi tayo makakapagpundar kung 'di ako kikilos (We won't be able to build a house if I don't move)," he reasoned.

It took Romeo two weeks and 600 pesos in capital to earn 20,000 pesos by selling shabu. A dutiful son, he turned the profit over to Lorna. He was shot dead a few days later, and with him died any hope of Lorna's eye operation. Two of Romeo's teenage children have since been left in Lorna's care. She currently divides her and her husband's income to pay for her medicines and to take care of the needs of the ten grandchildren who now live with them in a small shanty in Barangay Welfareville, Mandaluyong.

Another woman, Janet, said that her son was killed while waiting for his girlfriend in front of the neighborhood PisoNet, a peso-a-minute internet shop popular in low-income communities. He was not a drug user nor was he on the drug list. The intended target was a woman named Barbie, a drug user. Barbie was in the PisoNet with her three small children so the killers thought twice about killing her there. Instead, the motorcycle assassins went for Janet's son. He left behind two children. At her age, Janet can only afford to raise one.

In a small barangay in Tondo, Harold, a social worker, expressed concern for the orphaned Tokhang children, especially the girls. The loss of the father also means the loss of a significant amount of income for the family. The surviving family members are then forced to do whatever it takes to survive—including letting the young girls prostitute themselves to truck drivers and laborers in Manila's port area.

PECKING ORDER

In any chicken coop, there exists a pecking order. The alpha rooster sits on the highest perch and gets the choicest morsels. He reinforces the social hierarchy of the coop by pecking and bullying the other chickens. In an all-hen coop, however, the alpha hen takes the role of the alpha rooster. The alpha hen is reportedly more aggressive, pecking and bullying the smallest and weakest hens, sometimes to death if the weaker hens are not separated immediately. When the weakest hen is taken from the coop, the alpha hen targets the next weakest, and then the next, so on and so forth to remain at the top of the coop. Being an alpha hen is also passed on across generations.

While orphaned children, mothers, and grandmothers grapple with the multiple effects of the drug war, there are also women who use their power and influence to propel violence. Women like Mocha Uson take the lead in spreading fake news not only regarding the drug war but also other policies of the Duterte administration. Sass Rogando Sasot has taken on a similar role online, justifying the murders as a necessary evil. Despite not being a government official, Sasot's reach via social media has made her a political influencer among her numerous followers. This has resulted in a number of unsavory actions, including "Oplan Cyber Tokhang" which aims to harass individuals and groups who speak out online against Duterte and his administration.

The pecking order in the drug war shows who is on top and how institutions who support the Government's implementation ensure the status quo. Across the bureaucracy, legislators and various officials are complicit in the drug war, enacting policies such as Oplan Tokhang and MASA MASID (Mamamayang Ayaw sa Anomalya, Mamamayang Ayaw sa iligal na Droga). Some of these institutions are led by women, such as the Public Attorney's Office (PAO). PAO Chief Presida Acosta defended the Philippine National Police during the Senate probe into the killing of 17-year-old Kian Delos Santos by Caloocan City policemen.

"Mawalang-galang na po kay Senator (Risa) Hontiveros, wala pong pronouncement ang PAO na may pattern dito. Uulitin ko po, walang polisiya ang gobyerno na pumatay nang walang awa (With all due respect to Senator Hontiveros, PAO has no pronouncement that there is a pattern here. I repeat, there is no government policy to kill without mercy)," Acosta said. A few weeks after the hearing, Kian's parents were photographed with President Duterte, raising their fists in the administration's salute. They have since been placed under the "protective" custody of the Department of Justice.

At the barangay level, discretion amongst kapitans and kagawads determines who lives and who dies once they submit the drug watchlist to the police and the City Anti-Drug Abuse Council (CADAC). Some officials such as Kagawad Angela acknowledge that they cannot change the drug war, focusing instead on a Kamustahan program for the youth. Along with three children of her own, Angela takes on the gargantuan task of protecting the children in her community from state-sanctioned violence. Her husband, the former barangay chairman, was an early victim of the drug war, gunned down not far from their home. Others such as Jane make it clear that they are simply implementing the President's orders. Jane rationalises the drug war by stating that the city is now more peaceful with the suspected drug addicts arrested or in rehab. When asked if she is aware about the number of drug-related extrajudicial killings in her city, she said there were none "because the police have not reported any deaths".

REVENGE FOR THE BROOD

While mother hens are protective of their children, the broody hen is notorious for taking its protectiveness to the next level. A hen is deemed broody when, after years of having her eggs collected before they hatch, she becomes aggressive. The broody hen's maternal instincts are put into overdrive in her desire to have her eggs finally hatch into chicks. The broody hen would also pluck out her own chest feathers to keep her clutch of eggs warm and moist. She attacks anyone who attempts to approach her nest, in the hope of deterring predators.

There are signs that mothers have had enough. Nanay X, a grieving mother from Caloocan, lost her 13-year old son to masked killers and visits the police station every day to ask for updates on his case. The killers who shot her son were never identified, much less arrested. A few months after his death, Nanay X came to the community parish priest to confess. Unable to sleep at night, she had been searching the internet for instructions on how to make a homemade bomb. Something to plant at the police station, she said. After all, no one cared about her son, who had since been classified as just another "collateral damage".

Lorna's grandchild and the eldest of Romeo's

surviving teenage sons has been saving up his daily school allowance to buy a gun. Lorna approves of her grandchild's anger. In fact, Lorna wants revenge on the snitch who pointed her son out to the police. "Putangina, banatan niyo na rin (Motherfucker, kill him too)," she swore. "Tanggalan niyo na ng ulo para makabawi tayo (Cut his head off so we're quits)."

It is traditional practice to put live chicks on the coffins of those who die violent, unresolved deaths. The little beaks and claws scratching the glass of the coffin invoke a form of women's magic. The unknown killers are cursed to be haunted by their actions, ghostly beaks pecking at their conscience. Springing from this local superstition, a group of mothers have been collecting chicks for all the drug war's dead. One chick for each death. The plan is to bring all 27,000 chicks to Camp Crame, a bold accusation against the faceless puppet-masters behind the masked killers on the loose. Two years later, many of the chicks have grown. Some have been eaten, but justice remains elusive.

Reprinted from UMAALMÁ, KUMIKIBÔ: essays on women and violence, *Gantala Press, 2018*

NANAY BINING

Bernandina Enriquez Mendoza
translated by Faye Cura

I was born on May 20, 1941. I grew up during the Japanese War. At that time, all we did was hide in our homes.

My father worked as an interpreter for the Japanese. Even if he was a farmer, he spoke seven languages. He was called "Teacher."

We hadn't gone to school. Farming was all we ever did. We paid taxes to the owner of the land. We would slash-and-burn by the river. We would cut wood called rahita, tie them in bunches and sell them as firewood.

We lived in a place called Kamaligan (Granary). That was where the residents of what was called Lupang Kano (American Land) gathered. I became a young woman there. Sometimes, we would go to Cavite City, where our relatives harvested salt. When we returned to Lupang Kano, we already had a sack of salt, enough to eat with rice.

After the war, here comes Mr. Ilao, roaming the place, buying plots of lands. Among the land sold was Kamaligan which was owned by Old Woman de la Torre. We neighbors went our own ways. I just slept for a bit, and the next day, the Ramoses already had an office in Lupang Kano.

I sold snacks to the sugarcane workers. Got married

to the driver-mechanic of the Ramoses. I was sixteen when I got married, twenty-eight when I became a mother.

My husband was infertile. My mother always said that it's hard not to have children when one grows old, so I should have children of my own. I ended up fooling around with the caretaker of the Ramoses, who was older than me by twenty years. The caretaker and I had two children.

This wasn't a secret to my husband and the neighbors. My husband and the father of my children even agreed to tell the children about their real father when the time came. The caretaker left to take care of his sick wife. Meanwhile, I grew close with the assistant of the sugarcane contractor (since Lupang Kano was a sugarcane farm then). We also had two children. My husband and I finally separated. He sold all of our properties and visited all the beerhouses in Cavite. He contracted herpes, and died.

Talking about the value of land, the story of Lupang Kano is the story of who I am. From the sugarcane truck, to the scaffolding, the railroad track, the path leading to the spring, all of those are linked to my life. My children learned to farm at a young age. I would till the land, and behind me were my two children, planting string beans. I would gather bananas, my son Omeng would carry them on his back and my daughter Miriam would carry them on her head.

I always tell my children, I brought you up properly,

even if people judged me. I used to sell vegetables in Zapote. I would leave at two in the morning, go home at two in the afternoon. At four o'clock, I would walk the railroad track to fetch my children from school.

So I get terribly hurt when my children are being defamed in this struggle for land. I am mortified that the ones putting them down are their own cousins. If I die, I die. But I know that my death would be worth it because my children are in the right.

My siblings have died in this struggle. I love my siblings and nieces/nephews, but I love my children more. If there are people who want to hurt my children, I shall give my life. To my kumpares, kumares, relatives, I ask that you think long and hard about what is right and wrong in this land struggle. The fight for this land is the fight of my family and all the families that lived on Kamaligan.

Translation of "Nanay Bining" in LUPANG RAMOS: Isang Kasaysayan, *Gantala Press, 2018*

SCOURGE ON THE FLESH

Melinda Babaran
translated by Faye Cura

I've been staring at the empty suitcase for a long time. I couldn't start packing. I didn't understand how I was feeling. Mixed emotions seemed to clash inside me, concealed behind my blank stare. Happy-sad, worried, scared.

Do you have time? Can you stay with me for a while? Let's chat.

I'm about to go home to the Philippines. My contract as a factory worker in a big company of Integrated Circuits here in Taiwan has ended. It's sad. Because I have to leave the country that has been my home for more than a decade. I have to leave the country where I have been truly free.

I would have been happy coming back to where I grew up. Seeing familiar faces of relatives and friends. Even if many ugly memories are slowly coming back, especially now that my homecoming is near. I would have been happy. But my father is there, so I'm scared.

Is it weird? I'm afraid of my own father.

You know, it's because he doesn't accept me. He doesn't accept that his daughter is a tomboy.[2] When did I know that I'm like this? I was only in Grade Four

---

2   In the Philippines, tomboy connotes "lesbian," specifically "butch" lesbians, unlike in American English where tomboy could simply mean "boyish."

when I knew that I was different. A girl classmate let me sit on her lap. I couldn't explain how I felt, but it was good. In the beginning, my father paid little attention to me. Maybe he was drowning in his own sorrow since my mother had just left to work abroad. And because he had to be a mother as well as a father, he focused on my younger siblings. I was ten years old then. I didn't need to be looked after, and my parents had already seen that I was independent.

Maybe that was why he didn't notice that all my playmates were boys. That instead of dolls, my toys were text cards, bottlecaps, spinning tops, and yoyos. I played all day under the sun running, playing patintero and tumbang preso. And when angered, I wouldn't hesitate to hurl myself against my opponents or throw punches, even if they were all boys. I was thirteen when he started commenting on my actions. I was so gruff, he said. I was already a young lady but all I did, he said, was play in the streets. And worse, all my playmates were boys!

Whenever he saw me playing in the streets, he would whip me with his belt. Heat would run across my skin when the hard belt landed on my arms, my legs, my back, leaving a welt. That would happen wherever I was struck, and often he would use the metal part of the belt to hit me. With the pain, it seemed like my skin and muscles were slowly being torn apart.

When he wasn't wearing a belt, he would use the wooden handle of the soft broom. Other times, it was a bamboo rattan stick. He would hit me anywhere. Even if I tried to hide in the corners of our house, he would run after me. He was too enraged to care that it was a child he was striking, as he swung the weapon in his hand.

Often, he was like a boxing champ with the speed and strength of his blows on my young body. It was as if he was hoping that each punch he landed on my face and body would soften my male heart.

At first, I would cry whenever my father battered me. I would ask myself, did I commit such a big sin, to be hurt like that by my own father? I also thought sometimes that maybe he wasn't my real father, because a true parent could not hurt his child like that. Eventually, I got used to it. Even his insulting and hurtful words, such as: people like me were pests in society. No tears came anymore whenever my father would hurt me. And I was hardened by each whip, flog, and punch that I received. I was strengthened by each pain in my flesh.

One day, my mother arrived from abroad. This put a pause to my father's beatings. But one early morning he came home drunk. He entered my room. I was sleeping soundly but woke suddenly when he kicked me. He told me many hurtful things. He pointed at my face, insulting me, saying that I was a pest. I just sat there with my head down. My jaw was clenched. I couldn't accept and swallow his insults. My fists were clenched as well but I couldn't fight back. I couldn't do anything but silently cry and repeatedly wish that he would stop. Suddenly, I felt a sharp thing pointed at my neck. It was an ice pick! My father said that he would kill me if I didn't change. By then my mother had woken up and she pushed him out of my room. But before he left, he stabbed the ice pick on the bed, between my legs.

That's when I knew that I had to leave that house. I needed to leave because it was my own father who was going to kill me. I told myself that I needed to be free.

That's why I landed here in Taiwan. I've been travelling back and forth here for many years now, and it has become my second home. My life has become peaceful, living and working here for more than a decade already. I'm free to show who I really am without anyone judging me. In this country, everyone is treated equally. Here, I'm accepted for who I am as long as I'm not hurting anyone. I don't feel the need to hide. Even at work, I don't feel any discrimination from the Taiwanese. In fact, I would often joke around with my male Taiwanese colleagues. We also go out often to have fun. I have received not one hurtful word or look while in this country. I don't need to be afraid, because no one will hurt me. My life here in Taiwan is happy. Everything is fine in my life.

But, as they say, nothing is permanent in this life. After several years, I need to go home. To the Philippines, my real home. But I'm afraid. I'm afraid to see my father.

Please bear with me, if I'm about to cry.

I'm afraid to see his face, weathered by the seasons. His sunken cheeks and dull eyes.

I'm afraid to see his once-strong body, now skin and bones.

I don't think I can see his arms that once flogged my body, and are now defeated by a serious illness. He has cirrhosis of the liver. It is eating him alive. The progression of the illness is so fast. It hasn't even been a year, but it has weakened him greatly.

I'm afraid to see the once high and mighty pillar of our home, who is now close to saying goodbye. The money that I sent every month is not enough to prevent age and disease weakening him.

I don't want to see my father like that. I couldn't take it. Because in spite of the welts he left on my body, he is still my father. And I love him so much in spite of his shortcomings as a parent, in spite of his non-acceptance of who I am. Even if each blow on my body hardened my male heart, I remain a daughter. I remain a child who loves her father and is ready to forgive.

I fear for my father. I fear that he'll be gone without knowing that I still love him very much, that I have long forgiven him and let the lashes he gave me heal. I'm more afraid to think that one day, I won't be able to see him anymore and that I couldn't even serve him since I was working in another country. If something bad happens to him, I think that the scourge on my heart would be more painful than those on the flesh I endured before.

I'm sorry, ha. Is my drama too long? Please bear with me. But thank you for listening. Somehow, I feel better. Sige, dude. I still have to pack.

Translation of "Latay sa Laman," Jury Award in the 2018 Taiwan Literature Award for Migrants,
http://tlam.sea.taipei/?p=3062

LOVE LIFE

Claire Damolan
translated by Faye Cura

I was twelve years old when I stopped going to school due to poverty. I saw how my mother was and pitied her. Our family lived in Peñarrubia, Abra. I always went to the farm to help plant rice and vegetables like upo, eggplant, and corn. At that time, there were a lot of spotted fish in the farm. I enjoyed catching these, and frogs. I lost interest in school because our family could not even buy school supplies.

It was December, when we were harvesting rice, when a visitor came. I heard that he's the nephew of my father with his second cousin. He asked me if I wanted to go with him. In my desire to see Manila, I said yes. On the day of our departure from Ilocos, I wondered why we were only riding a jeep. I thought that one had to take the bus to go to Manila. I couldn't do anything but cry.

When we arrived at their house in Baay, Abra, I realized that my work there was harder than that at the farm. I became the caretaker of two children, one boy (five years old) and one girl (three years old). I worked at a house beside a river. We bathed in the river and that was also where I learned to swim, so I'll never forget that place.

One day, a former neighbor saw me. She asked why

I was there and if I wanted to go home. I immediately said yes. She said that she was going to tell my mother so they could fetch me. After several months, I saw my eldest sibling coming towards the house. I felt immense joy. At last, I could leave this mountain. And that's what happened; I went home.

After only three months, someone was looking for a housemaid in Manila, and I was asked if I wanted the job. I said yes. We left the next day. This time, we rode the bus, so I said, this is the real deal, I'm really going to Manila. Finally I'll be able to see the different colors of the city.

We arrived in Manila after almost a whole day's journey. I was brought to a place called Sampaloc, to the house of my employers. The man was a dentist while the woman worked at the Department of Justice. They had four children. The family was good to me. But sometimes, they lacked money. I was fifteen years old then and my wages were 30 pesos a month. That was a big amount in those days. You could buy a lot of things because the value of the peso was high in 1970. You could buy a dress in Quiapo for 10 pesos.

After seven months of working for the family, I decided to leave since they could not pay my wages any more. I found a new employer in Makati, and my wages were 50 pesos a month. I lasted for only two months because there were a lot of people in the house, and the house was massive. We were three housemaids.

My third employer was from Parang, Marikina, a

colonel at Camp Crame. We were also three housemaids, and they trained me to cook for the household. They had three children, two young men and one young woman. We three housemaids were always left at home. I went to the market every Sunday with my woman employer. I carried the two bayongs in both hands. We always went to the church first to hear mass. I lasted two and a half years with them. That was where I was when Martial Law was declared in 1972. I got fed up working and decided to go home to our town.

I idled about until one day a neighbor came to tell me that her brother needed a cook in Manila. Her brother lived alone so I agreed. We returned to Manila. We arrived at my future employer's house at night. My hair was long then, down to my hips. "Who's that long-haired young woman with you?" my future employer asked. "She's the one I brought here to stay with you, the one I chose to be your wife," his sister answered. I heard what the sister said loud and clear, but I didn't think much of it. The next day, the sister returned to the province, leaving me in that house.

One night, while we were watching TV, my employer asked if I had a boyfriend. I told him I didn't. "So, that means I can court you? I'll be frank. I really like you. The moment I saw you, it's like my manhood came to life. Many women volunteer to be my wife but I don't feel anything for them. You're the only one who made the hair on my arms rise," he told me. "So if you'll agree, let's get married. We'll go to America if you like."

I told him no, and also that I did not want to go to America. He asked, "Why not? The other women who come here ask me to marry them and take them to America."

One night, he couldn't contain himself and he hugged me. I ran. He chased me around the table. After some time, he got tired and stopped running after me. He apologized afterwards. I cried, not because I was scared of him but because I was so angry at him, especially whenever I saw his bald head.

That December, I went on a vacation to Abra. My friends and I went to the farm to harvest rice. He followed me there and asked me to come back to Manila. I told him that I did not want to go back anymore. He didn't force me, but after Christmas he came again. He brought my uncle, his childhood friend, to talk to me.

"Why don't you want to marry him? Aren't you tired of being poor? Don't you want to be comfortable in life?" my uncle asked. At first I still wouldn't say yes, but they continued to persuade me until finally I acquiesced.

I married him. We had three children. My husband died in 1982 of a heart attack. From then on, I have served as both mother and father to our children.

Translation of "Love Life" in DALOY: A collection of writings from the Filipino migrant women of Batis AWARE, *Batis Association of Women in Action for Rights and Empowerment, 2018*

BEMBARAN O ALONGAN

Elin Anisha Guro

Dear Inged a Pilombayan ami a Bembaran o Alongan,

Alamat sorat kami o manga wata aka, melagid den so miyakapoon reka ago so matag ka tiyagikor ago pimbabawata den.

We are coming home to you, bolawan ami. Please do not worry that the Torogan is in such complete disarray. We already know what happened. We saw everything from a distance, but the huge fire kept us from rushing to your side.

Mataya ami a inged, you may now be in ruins, but we will come home to you still. We will make columns, beams, walls, and floors out of the mountains of debris. We will make roofs out of our tattered malong remnants so we can quickly rebuild our homes. We will work faster than the airstrikes that bombed our houses.

Your displaced children will embrace you with their compassion and humanity. No, our beloved city, we will not blame you, we will not judge you, but we ask for your forgiveness. Perila-i kami ngka. Forgive us—for the sins of the few. They are to blame for your suffering, your near-death. May we never forget the unburied bodies. May we learn from the intensity and severity of this siege. May we unmask the faces of those among us who fed and prospered on the abject poverty and ignorance of the many.

We are coming home. Our bleeding hearts and lasting memories will help us navigate the labyrinth that you have become. We will be raising a yellow flag. Not white, because we did not surrender you. Nor will we ever accept your death. Not black because we have never welcomed foreign ideology, not 500 years ago and not now. Our flag is yellow because it symbolises the ancient Meranaw royalty and Pat a Pengampong ko Ranao that runs in the blood of every single Meranaw. We hope to remember what made us Meranaws all through these centuries and we hope to keep our religion, Islam. It is yellow because you are the Bembaran o Alongan, the Kingdom Where the Sun Rises. No matter how long this storm lasts, the sun will one day rise on the Bembaran o Alongan.

The same blood that was shed with wanton abandon and used to defray the cost of this tragic lesson will re-bind us. We will meet the breaking sun as it showers its rays on the Sleeping Lady while the ancient Lake Lanao reflects those beams. Lake Lanao is testimony of the resilience of our people who existed long before the consciousness of a nation was born, a nation carved out from the tears and blood of our ancestors, from the theft of our land and our resources. The Sleeping Lady is both the witness to our unspeakable agony and the symbol of our unshakable strength and endurance.

We will come home to you no matter what it takes, no matter how long it takes. The Bembaran o Alongan shall not fail as long as the sun rises.

Reprinted from LAWANEN: Mga Alaala ng Pagkubkob, Mga Haraya ng Pag-igpaw, *Gantala Press, 2018*

ABOUT THE CONTRIBUTORS

Natalie Pardo Labang is a graduate of the University of the Philippines. She is from the province of Camarines Norte.

Elizabeth Ruth Deyro is a Pushcart Prize-nominated poet, freelance journalist, and literary editor from the province of Laguna.

Roda Tajon is a transgender woman and is currently working on her degree in women and development.

Kristine Ong Muslim is the author of nine books, co-editor of two anthologies, and translator of various works. She grew up and continues to live in a rural town in southern Philippines.

Christine Marie Lim Magpile is taking her MA in

Philippine Studies at the University of the Philippines. She currently works as a copy editor at the UP Press.

Carissa Natalia Baconguis took up her BFA in Creative Writing at the Ateneo de Manila University. She is the author of the poetry collection, *Euridice at ang Paghahanap kay Bathala*.

Kaisa Aquino is currently writing a collection of short stories for her master's thesis in Malikhaing Pagsulat (Creative Writing) at the University of the Philippines. She was born and raised in the province of Isabela.

China Pearl Patria De Vera is finishing her graduate studies at the University of the Philippines. She is a teacher, a senior editor at Aklat Alamid, and aunt to Pachochoy.

Liberty A. Notarte-Balanquit is an Assistant Professor at the Department of Humanities, College of Arts and Sciences, University of the Philippines Los Baños. She lives in the City of Los Baños, province of Laguna with Tony and their daughters, Bulan and Siday.

After 30 years of employment as a domestic helper in Europe then as an administrative professional at the International Food Policy Research Institute (IFPRI) and The World Bank in Washington, DC, multilingual *Yolanda F. Catalla (Palis)* is back in the City of Los

Baños, the Philippines. Her works appear in the anthologies *Returning a Borrowed Tongue, Babaylan,* and more recently in Gantala Press' *Danas.* Yoli owns and manages Books, Crafts, and Coffeeshop, a second-hand bookstore where oddities may be found and where emerging writers, playwrights, budding poets, and shy composers can present their creative work.

Karla Quimsing is from Iloilo City but spent most of her professional life in Cebu City. Her literary works include *Pansit Poetry* (2016), *Tingog Nanay* (2017), and *Isla* (2018). She currently resides in Paris with her husband Francis and their two children, Isla and Kanta.

Miriam Villanueva is a peasant leader and officer of Katipunan ng mga Lehitimong Magsasaka at Mamamayan sa Lupang Ramos, an organization that struggles for the right to till agricultural land in the City of Dasmariñas, province of Cavite.

Faye Cura is a writer, editor, and founder/publisher of Gantala Press. She is the author of three poetry collections.

Rae Rival is a co-founder of Gantala Press. She volunteers for the Amihan National Federation of Peasant Women and Rural Women Advocates.

Melanie dela Cruz was a repacker at Regent Foods Corporation (RFC), where she had worked for 24 years. She was among the workers arrested and jailed following a violent dispersal by police and goons of the month-long strike against RFC in November 2019.

Estrelita "Ka Inday" Bagasbas is an urban poor leader of Kalipunan ng Damayang Mahihirap (Kadamay). Originally from the province of North Cotabato in southern Philippines, she comes from a family of farmers. From her savings as a domestic helper in Yemen, she was able to build a house in Barangay San Roque, Quezon City, Metro Manila, a community about to be bulldozed to give way to condominiums and a casino.

Organisasyon dagiti Nakurapay nga Umili ti Syudad (ORNUS) is an organization of the urban poor in Baguio City, northern Philippines.

Judy Cariño is a cultural worker, writer, and editor who focuses on the indigenous knowledge and culture of the Cordillera indigenous peoples. Among her recent works is the book, *Heirloom Recipes of the Cordillera.*

Eileen R. Tabios has released about 60 collections of poetry, fictions, essays, and experimental biographies in nine countries and cyberspace. Her body of work includes invention of the hay(na)ku poetic form as well as a first poetry book, *Beyond Life Sentences* (1998), which received the National Book Award for Poetry. She has edited, co-edited, or conceptualized 15 anthologies of poetry, fiction, and essays as well as exhibited visual art and poetry in the US, Asia, and Serbia.

Priscilla Supnet Macansantos, a Mathematician by profession, writes poetry and nonfiction in English, Filipino and Iloco. She was editor in chief of University of the Philippines Baguio's student publication, the *Outcrop*, during Martial Law; later devoted time in administration (as UP Baguio Chancellor until 2012); and was Head of the National Commission for Culture and the Arts's Literary Arts Committee for three years.

Dumay Solinggay is a Kankanaey poet whose home city is Baguio. She is currently based in Ha Noi where she teaches English to pre-schoolers.

Ilay L. Quidangen is an Itneg-Ilocano transplant in Baguio City.

Ica Fernandez, *Abbey Pangilinan*, and *Mixkaela Villalon* are members of Sandata, a collaborative collective composed of researchers and artists responding to the spate of disinformation in the context of the Philippine Drug War. They have been working together since 2016 and have released multiple streams of work including papers, presentations, and the *Kolateral* music album.

Bernandina "Bining" Enriquez Mendoza was born and raised in Lupang Ramos, a 372-hectare agricultural land/former hacienda in the City of Dasmariñas, province of Cavite. She is a member of Katipunan ng mga Lehitimong Magsasaka at Mamamayan sa Lupang Ramos.

Melinda Babaran has been working as a factory worker in Taiwan for 12 years now. In 2018, she won the Jury Award at the Taiwan Literature Award for Migrants for her essay titled "Latay sa Laman."

Claire Damolan is a member of Batis AWARE (Association of Women in Action for Rights and Empowerment), a self-help people's organization of Filipino migrant women. She is from Caloocan City, Metro Manila.

Scholar, educator, and culture-bearer *Elin Anisha Guro*'s lifelong dedication to the educational empowerment of her fellow Meranaws, the preservation of their culture, and the protection of Lake Lanao in the Islamic City of Marawi, southern Philippines, from which they derive their identity as "People of the Lake" informs her poetry, blog, advocacy, and politics.

Copyright © the authors 2020
Translations copyright © the translators 2020

This edition published in the United Kingdom by Tilted Axis Press in 2020. This translation was funded by Arts Council England and 198 brilliant Kickstarter backers. Thank you!

tiltedaxispress.com

The rights of the authors and translators of these works to be identified as such have been asserted in accordance with Section 77 of the Copyright, Designs and Patent Act 1988.

This is a work of fiction. Names, characters, places and incidents are either the product of the author's imagination or are used fictitiously. Any resemblance to any actual persons, living or dead, events or locales is entirely coincidental.

ISBN (chapbook)   9781911284529
ISBN (ebook)   9781911284512

A catalogue record for this book is available from the British Library.

Cover design by Soraya Gilanni Viljoen
Typesetting and ebook production by Simon Collinson
Printed and bound by Footprint Workers Co-op, Leeds

Supported using public funding by
ARTS COUNCIL ENGLAND